Start to
Quilt

Miriam Edwards

SEARCH PRESS

First published in paperback in Great Britain 2008
Search Press Ltd
Wellwood
North Farm Road
Tunbridge Wells
Kent TN2 3DR

Reprinted 2010

First published in hardback by Search Press Ltd 2007

Text copyright © Miriam Edwards 2007

Photographs by Charlotte de la Bédoyère, Search Press Studios and by Roddy Paine Photographic Studios Thanks to V & A Images, Victoria and Albert Museum for the quilt photograph on page 4

Photographs and design copyright © Search Press Ltd 2007

ISBN: 978-1-84448-389-1

The Publishers and authors can accept no responsibility for any consequences arising from the information, advice or instructions given in this publication.

Suppliers
If you have difficulty obtaining any of the materials and equipment mentioned in this book, please visit the Search Press website for details of suppliers:
www.searchpress.com

> Some words are underlined <u>like this</u>. They are explained in the glossary on page 48.

For Chris, my teacher, my inspiration and above all my friend.

Acknowledgements

A big thanks for the support of friends and family. Also to Michelle, Corin and Trevor for teaching me to use the computer (and rescuing me when it went wrong), and to Roy, my husband, for being there for me. To my maternal grandfather and his sisters, who all sewed for pleasure and a living, and to my Mum who created magic with her needle and thread.

Thanks also to Sue Trangmar of Daisy Chain Designs for the lovely felts I used; Yvette Ness for the butterfly fabric and beads; and Anne Roberts of Out of Africa for her gift of lovely threads to jazz up the quilting and Valerie for teaching me her glove stitch. Lastly the biggest thanks go to Christine Reid for introducing me to the joy of quilting in her classes and giving me the confidence to fly.

The publishers would like to thank the following for appearing in the photographs:
Lucia Brisefer, Katherine Chandrain, Charlie de la Bédoyère, Nicole Fields and Katrina Hindley.

Printed in Malaysia

Contents

Introduction   4

Materials   6

Techniques   10

Notebook Cover   14

Fun Phone Pouch   18

Sashiko Bag   26

Beady Bag   32

Cat Wall Hanging   38

More books to read   48

Glossary   48

Index   48

Introduction

Quilting is the art of sewing together three layers: backing, padding and then top fabric. You make a 'quilt sandwich' and then join the layers together with stitches or with ties, buttons or beads.

Quilting began in Asia before the first century AD. Europeans discovered it around 1099 when Christian crusaders went to fight the Turks in the Middle East, and saw that they were wearing light-weight quilted armour.

In Europe in the Middle Ages, people wore quilted clothes and used lap quilts to keep out the cold. In the rich houses and castles, large wall hangings helped to keep in the heat.

During the 1500s, quilts were made using fine silks from the East. Quilting remained especially popular in the north of England and Wales. In the north of England, miners' wives would sew for an extra income. The patterns were handed down from mother to daughter. In Wales the quilter was often a single lady who would travel from farm to farm.

FUNKY FACT!

In the Middle Ages, soldiers wore quilted clothes under their armour to stop the metal from rubbing their skin.

When pioneers left England for America, they took the craft with them, and it continued to develop. Small pieces of cloth were sewn together to form a patchwork block. When enough blocks had been made, the pioneer women would meet to sew them together and quilt them.

A patchwork quilt from the 1760s.

I have always enjoyed sewing. My mother, aunts and even my grandfather all sewed so as a child I was always surrounded by lovely colourful fabrics and textures. My mother taught me to sew clothes for my dolls, myself and later my own children. I joined a class and soon became addicted to quilting and patchwork. Later I was asked to start teaching children to sew and quilt, which has been a wonderful experience.

I hope you will enjoy the projects in this book twice over: once when you are making them and again when you see the lovely results!

Materials

Fabric and wadding

Choose colours and fabrics you would like to work with, as you will spend time and energy on your project and you want to look at it with love and pride. I usually use 100 per cent cotton as it does not fray and slip like other fabrics. When you are more experienced, you can experiment with all kinds of fabrics. Always wash and iron your fabric before using it. This takes out all the chemicals, and if the colour is going to run it is better to find out now. For some projects you will want to quilt around shapes or patterns on the top fabric, so choose one with a good design.

Felt can be fun for decorating quilted projects. I have used it for the flowers on the Notebook Cover on page 14 and for the cat in the Cat Wall Hanging on page 38.

In shadow quilting, the design is attached to the background fabric and a lightweight, transparent fabric is placed on top. You then stitch round the design, attaching the layers together. I have used a sheer fabric called voile for the top fabric but you can also use net.

Use low loft polyester wadding for the padding layer of your quilt projects. I have also used a cotton mix of eighty per cent cotton and twenty per cent polyester (80/20) for the Cat Wall Hanging because it is flatter. Note that in the US, wadding is called 'batting'.

TOP TIP!

If you choose a fabric but the colour runs when you wash it, put a handful of cooking salt in the rinse water. Soak it for half an hour, then rinse it. Pat it with a white cloth. If it still loses colour, choose another fabric!

Fabrics, wadding and felt for your quilted projects.

Sewing equipment

I quilt with a big eye no. 10 needle. This is a small needle, so it helps make small stitches, but it has a big eye, which makes it easy to thread. For bigger stitches or thicker thread, I use an embroidery needle, a no. 7 with a sharp point. Buy a packet of mixed needles so that you can find one that is right for you.

You can use special quilting thread for quilting. It is cotton wrapped in polyester and comes in a rainbow of colours, either to match your work or to contrast. When you are sewing seams, normal sewing thread is fine. Use a cream colour on light fabrics and a grey on dark fabrics, as these will blend in with most colours. For decorative stitches, use coton à broder or perlé, or thicker threads if you really want the stitches to show up. I have used thick, variegated thread in many of the projects. I have also used variegated crochet cotton.

Choose fine, long pins that you can see easily. Fine pins will not damage your fabric. Use a pincushion to keep them safe. Use a thimble to protect your fingers when sewing.

A sewing machine is used for some of the projects in this book. Ask an adult to help you.

Use embroidery scissors for cutting threads, a large sharp pair for cutting fabric, and pinking shears where you want a fancy edge. Do not use your fabric scissors for cutting paper or card.

Fabric scissors, pinking shears and embroidery scissors.

Thick, variegated cotton perlé threads, normal sewing thread, quilting thread, a thimble, a pincushion and a ball of thick crochet cotton.

7

Decorative bits and pieces

Ribbons A narrow ribbon is used for the Cat Wall Hanging (see page 38). Collect lots of different ribbons to decorate your quilting.

Buttons Look in someone's button box for interesting buttons, such as flower shapes. Shops that sell fabric also have a plenty of lovely buttons in different shapes, colours and sizes.

Beads Seed beads look beautiful on quilted projects, and they are easy to sew on.

Florist wire This is used for making flower arrangements, but it is really useful for all kinds of crafts. You can buy it in florist's shops. I have used turquoise florist wire to make fun spirals for the Cat Wall Hanging.

Decorative threads These are sold in mixed bags of threads in different textures that blend in beautifully together. I have used red decorative threads for the belt that goes with the Sashiko Bag (see page 31).

Beaded trim These are great for finishing off projects. I used a green one to decorate a book cover that goes with the Notebook Cover project (see page 17).

Seed beads, buttons, ribbon, a beaded trim, decorative threads and florist wire.

Other equipment

Iron This is used to prepare fabric for quilting, to press folds in it and to apply fusible web to it.

Card You will need this to make templates.

Pencil This is used for drawing and tracing.

Washable felt pens These are ideal for drawing on fabric because they wash out in a cool wash.

Permanent marker You can use this to draw on felt or other fabrics.

Chalk markers These are useful for marking dark fabrics, as in the Sashiko Bag project (see page 26). The chalk brushes off later.

Fusible web This is used to attach one piece of fabric to another.

Tape measure This is used to measure fabric and embellishments. A **ruler** can also be used.

Safety pins These can be used to keep your quilt sandwich together while you work on it, as in the Beady Bag project (see page 32).

Fabric adhesive spray This is used in the Cat Wall Hanging (see page 38) to stick the layers of the quilt sandwich together before quilting. It should be used in a well-ventilated room. Read the instructions carefully.

Press stud A press stud is used to fasten the Fun Phone Pouch on page 18.

Sticky tape This is used to tape down patterns.

Compasses These are used for drawing circles.

Old scissors These are for cutting florist wire.

Notebook You make a cover for this in the Notebook Cover project.

Bag handles These are used in the Sashiko Bag project.

Dowelling This is used for the Cat Wall Hanging.

Fabric adhesive spray, sticky tape, an iron, a notebook, compasses, a chalk marker, washable pens, a pencil and permanent marker, dowelling, safety pins, old scissors, bag handles, fusible web, a press stud, tape measure, ruler and card.

Techniques

✳ Making a quilt sandwich

Place the backing fabric face down on the table, then the wadding on top of that, then the top fabric right side up on top. This forms a quilt sandwich. This is either spray glued together, as in the Cat Wall Hanging, or tacked with large stitches, or pinned with safety pins so that it stays firm while you sew the quilt together.

A quilt sandwich showing (left to right) the top fabric, wadding and backing fabric.

✳ Starting and finishing running stitch

Running stitch is used to sew the layers of the quilt together.

1 Thread your needle as shown.

2 Knot the end of the thread and put the needle through from the back to the front of the fabric.

3 Pull the thread through from the back. Pick up several running stitches at once on the needle.

4 Pull the thread through to show the running stitches. Continue to the end of the row.

5 Put the needle through to the back. Put the needle through a stitch as shown, but not through the fabric.

6 Go through the next stitch in the other direction.

7 Cut off the end of the thread. The thread is now secured at the back.

✳ Overstitch

This is used for sewing two edges together, as in the Sashiko Bag on page 24.

1 Knot the end of the thread. About 1cm (3/8in) from where you want to start, come up from the back to the front of the front fabric only. Pull through to bury the knot between the edges.

2 Go in from the back and out to the front where you came out before. Pull the thread through.

3 First you need to secure the beginning of the stitching. Do three diagonal stitches towards the left-hand side as shown.

4 Cross over the first three stitches with three more diagonal stitches towards the right.

5 Continue stitching to sew the edges together. Then go back over two stitches towards the left to secure the end of the stitching.

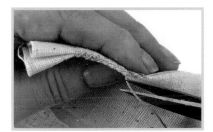

6 Trim the end of the thread.

✳ Slip stitch

This stitch is used to sew hems. You will need slip stitch to attach the handles on the Sashiko Bag.

1 Tie a knot. Make a little stitch in the backing fabric.

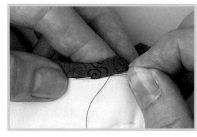

2 Pull the thread through. Fold the hem under as shown. Take up a bit of the edge of the hem.

3 Pull through. Underneath the hem, take up a tiny bit of the backing fabric and go into the hem again. Continue as shown.

☀ Tie and buttons

This technique can be used to hold your quilt together, either with running stitches or instead of them. It makes patterns and designs on your quilt, as on the Cat Wall Hanging.

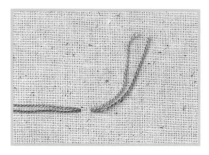

1 Double the thread. Go down and come up again, leaving a tail.

2 Go down and come up again in the same holes as before.

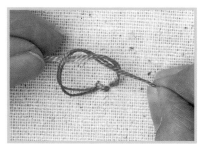

3 Pull the needle through, trim the end to match the tail and tie a knot, right over left.

4 Pull the knot tight and tie another knot, this time left over right.

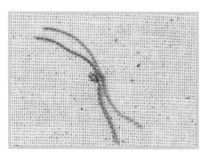

5 Pull the second knot tight and trim the ends.

☀ Adding buttons

To add a button, the steps are the same, but with a button in place as shown.

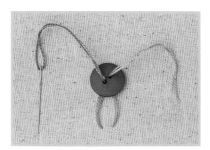

1 Go down and up through the holes in the button.

2 Do steps 2 to 4 as before, but with the button in place.

✳ Glove stitch

This stitch is a strong, decorative way of joining together two raw edges of felt or fabric. It is an alternative to blanket stitch.

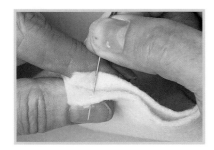

1 Knot the end. Work from left to right. As for overstitch, come up from the back to the front of the front fabric only. This will hide the knot.

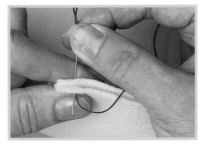

2 Next go from the back through both back and front fabrics.

3 Pull the thread through. Go diagonally 1.3cm (½in) along to the right and go through the back and front fabrics again.

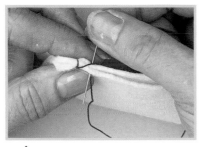

4 Go through once again to finish the stitch.

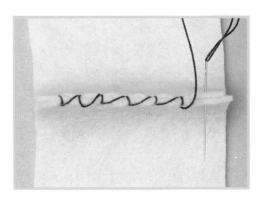

A row of glove stitch worked.

✳ Blanket stitch

This is a way of edging a raw edge of wool or fabric, as on a blanket. I have used it as a decorative way of attaching flowers in the Cat Wall Hanging.

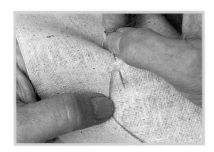

1 Come up at the bottom left and make a stitch going downwards.

2 Pull the thread through, then hold it down with your thumb as shown. Make another stitch downwards.

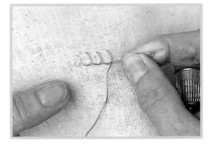

3 Pull through and continue to stitch in the same way. To finish off, take the needle through to the back just underneath the last loop.

Notebook Cover

You will need

- A5 notebook
- Pale pink felt, 45.7cm (18in) square
- Purple felt, 25.5cm (10in) square
- Cream felt, 12.7cm (5in) square
- Scraps of yellow, bright pink, blue and green felt for flowers
- Sheer voile, 15.2cm (6in) square
- Pins, needles and fabric scissors
- Thick purple thread
- Thick, variegated pink/purple crochet cotton
- Cotton sewing thread in yellow and black
- Three flower buttons
- Card, 10cm (4in) square
- A4 card for templates
- Washable felt tip pen

Shadow quilting is a very old technique, dating back to the 1700s. It is believed to have come from India. It is a way of attaching small pieces of fabric to a background when the pieces are too small to sew. You sew a piece of see-through fabric over the pieces to hold them in place. This tones down the colours of the pieces of fabric like a shadow and creates a soft, dreamy effect.

The pattern for the Notebook Cover, shown full size. Photocopy the design and tape the photocopy to a sheet of card. Cut round the shapes to make card templates of the flowers and stalks.

I Take scraps of yellow, bright pink, blue and green felt. Hold a flower template on to a piece of felt and cut round it. Cut round the stalk templates on dark green felt.

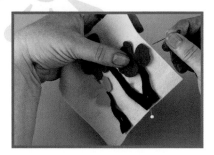

2 Pin the pieces in place on the cream felt. Pin from the back, as this stops your thread from becoming caught in the pins.

3 Place the voile square over the felt square and pin it in place. Thread a needle with yellow cotton and sew around the flower design in running stitch.

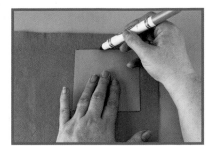

4 Cut the pale pink felt to 33 x 23cm (13 x 9in). Take the card square and place it 2.5cm (1in) down and 2.5cm (1in) in from the top right-hand corner. Draw round it using washable felt tip pen.

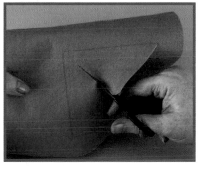

5 Cut out the square. Start in the middle and cut out diagonally to the corners, then cut round the edges.

6 Trim the voile to the edges of the cream felt square.

7 Place the pink felt with the window over the shadow quilted panel and pin it in place.

8 Thread a needle with the variegated crochet cotton. Start 3mm (1/8in) from the edge of the window, at the bottom left-hand corner. Leave a 7.5cm (3in) tail and sew round the window with large running stitches.

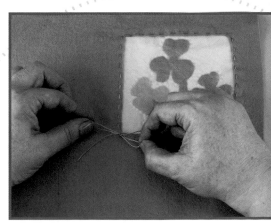

9 Leave a 7.5cm (3in) tail at the end and tie the two tails in a bow.

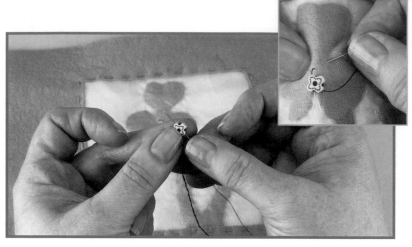

_10_ Use black thread to sew the buttons to the flower centres. Knot the thread, come up from the back and go through the button. Then go down near to where you came up. Go through all the layers of the shadow quilting. Repeat three times.

_11_ Secure each button at the back of the quilting with a couple of stitches.

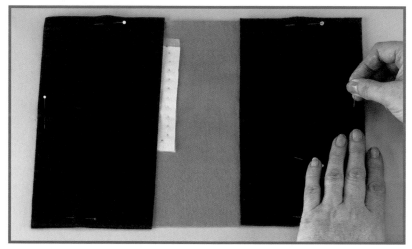

_13_ Using the thick purple thread, stitch round all four edges of the notebook cover in glove stitch (see page 13).

_12_ Turn over the book cover. Cut two rectangles from the purple felt, each one 12.7 x 23cm (5 x 9in). Pin them in place as shown.

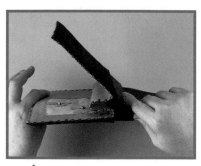

_14_ Open your notebook and push the front and back covers into the purple pockets of the notebook cover as shown.

The finished Notebook Cover would look great on your school journal, a sketchbook, address book or diary.

What next?

Book covers make great gifts for your friends. Try different colours and designs, and add beads and sequins.

Fun Phone Pouch

This funky pouch is made using the Japanese folded patchwork technique, which is based on the paper folding art of origami. The pouch has a handy belt attachment and you could use it to hold your glasses, sunglasses or spare change instead of a phone.

1 Use compasses to draw one 11.4cm (4½in) diameter circle and one 12.7cm (5in) circle on card. Cut the circles out.

2 Use a pencil to draw round the 12.7cm (5in) circle on the back of the pink fabric. Draw and cut out four circles.

3 Thread a needle with quilting thread and knot the end. Sew in running stitch round the edge of a circle. Do not cut the thread.

4 Place the pink circle right side down and place the 11.4cm (4½in) card circle in the centre.

5 Pull the thread tight to gather the edges of the pink fabric circle as shown.

6 Put in a couple of stitches to secure the end, then trim the thread. Make three more circles following steps 3 to 6. Turn the circles over and press them with an iron.

Stay Safe!
Always have an adult with you when you are ironing.

7 Bend the card templates so that you can remove them from the circles.

8 Cut a 7.6cm (3in) square from card. Draw round it on the back of the turquoise fabric four times. Cut out four squares.

9 Cut out four 7.6cm (3in) squares of wadding in the same way. Place a gathered fabric circle wrong side up, then a square of wadding, then a turquoise square right side up, making a small quilt sandwich.

10 Fold the top of the circle down over the top of the square as shown and pin it in place.

11 Fold and pin the other sides of the circle as shown.

12 Thread the needle with thick variegated thread and knot the end. Come up under the corner of a pink flap to hide the knot.

13 Sew in large running stitches round the edges of the flaps, through all the layers.

14 When you reach the end of one flap, make a stitch over the corner to begin the next flap.

15 The finished square, right side up. Make four squares in the same way, following steps 9 to 14.

16 Place two of the squares right sides together. Sew them together along one edge, using overstitch (see page 11). This is the front of the phone pouch.

18 Pin the layers together. Thread a needle with the thick variegated thread and knot the end. Go down on the inside of the sandwich and come up on the outside, to hide the knot.

17 Cut rectangles 14.5 x 4cm (5¾ x 1½in) from turquoise fabric, pink fabric and wadding. Trim one end to a point as shown to make tab shapes. Make a quilt sandwich with a turquoise tab shape right side down, a wadding tab shape and a pink tab shape right side up.

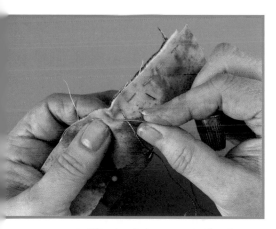

19 Sew in large running stitch round the edge of the tab. Make sure your stitches are neat on the turquoise side, since this will show.

20 Lay one quilted square right side up and lay the tab on top, turquoise side down, as shown. The top of the tab should be 6mm (¼in) above the top of the square.

21 Place the last quilted square right side down on top as shown.

22 Pin the top edge and overstitch it (see page 11) using pink cotton.

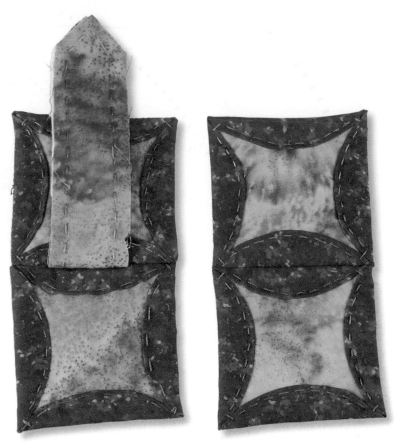

The back and front of the phone pouch should now look like this, right sides up.

23 Put the back on top of the front, right sides together. Pin the left-hand side. Pin the right-hand side up to the top of the bottom square.

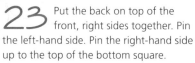

24 Using pink thread, overstitch (see page 11) down the whole left-hand side, across the bottom and up one square only of the right-hand side.

25 Turn the phone pouch right-side out.

26 Fold the tab up and over the top to the front of the phone pouch. Mark with a pin where the tab will need to be fastened to the pouch.

27 Lift the tab and place a second pin in the pouch. This shows where the base of the press stud will go.

29 Sew on the press stud parts. Use pink thread for the tab, turquoise for the pouch. Hide the knot under the stud and overstitch in and out of the holes.

28 Place the two parts of the press stud as shown.

30 Sew on the flower button. Knot the thread and come up from the back under the button, so that the knot is hidden. Then sew several times through the holes in the button, and finish off with a couple of stitches at the back.

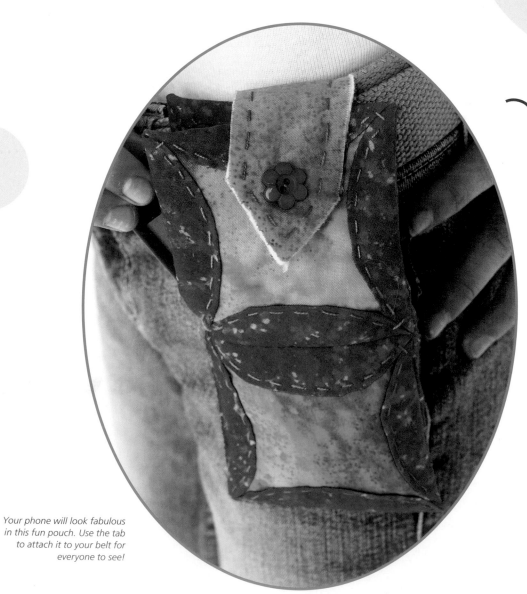

Your phone will look fabulous in this fun pouch. Use the tab to attach it to your belt for everyone to see!

What next?

Why not sew twelve blocks together, making four rows of three, and use it as a lovely make-up bag. You could even make a clutch bag.

Sashiko Bag

Sashiko means 'little stabs' or running stitch. In Japan in the early 1900s, the wives of farmers and fishermen used to make them warm, protective clothes by sewing together layers of cloth. Later, white thread was used on dark blue, indigo-dyed cloth, in many different patterns. Sashiko was used to sew firemen's protective coats. The patterns were worn on the inside for fighting fires, and on the outside for parades. This pattern is called *seigaiha* or 'waves'.

The pattern for the Sashiko Bag, shown half size. Enlarge it to 200 per cent on a photocopier.

1 Photocopy and enlarge the pattern, then cut out the insides of the wave shapes as shown.

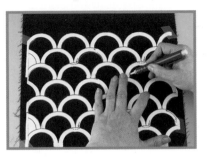

2 Tape the pattern to a navy cotton square. Draw round the pattern with the chalk marker.

3 Place the patterned navy piece on top of the calico square.

4 Pin the navy fabric to the calico. Thread a needle with the thick orange variegated thread and knot the end. Leaving the knot at the back, come up at the bottom right-hand side of the pattern. Begin stitching the design in running stitch.

5 When you come to the bottom of a wave shape, go through to the back and come up as shown to begin the next wave shape along.

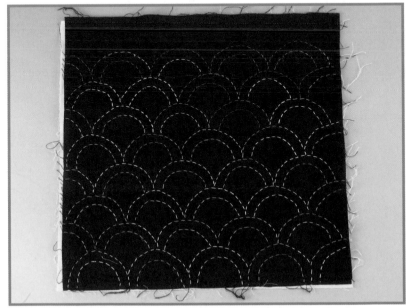

6 Continue stitching the waves from right to left. Stitch all the orange waves first, then thread the needle with the thick variegated blue thread and stitch the blue waves. Remove the pins.

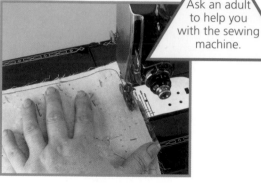

Stay Safe!
Ask an adult to help you with the sewing machine.

TOP TIP!
If you sew rounded corners, as I have here, the bag will end up nice and square when you turn it right sides out.

7 Place the stitched navy square right side up on the table. Place a blue lining square on top, right side down. Pin it in place.

8 Using a sewing machine, begin sewing 10cm (4in) from the top right-hand corner. Sew down to the bottom right-hand corner and sew round the corner.

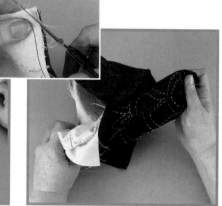

9 Sew along the bottom and up the second side, stopping 10cm (4in) from the top. Take out the pins.

10 Trim round the corners using fabric scissors. Then turn the bag front right sides out.

11 Place the navy square for the bag back on the table, and the blue lining square on top, right side down.

12 Use the sewing machine to sew the back exactly as you did the front: start 10cm (4in) from the top, sew down the side, along the bottom and up the other side to 10cm (4in) from the top. Trim the corners.

13 Turn the bag back right sides out. Place the bag front on top of the bag back, right sides together.

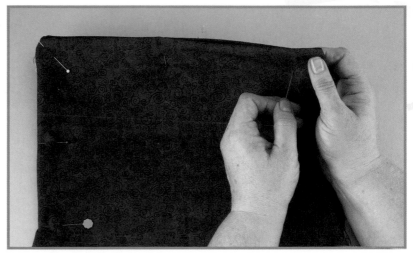

14 Carefully pin together the machine-stitched edges of the bag, leaving the top 10cm (4in) unpinned.

15 Use the sewing machine to sew the back and front of the bag together, leaving the top 10cm (4in) unstitched on both sides as before.

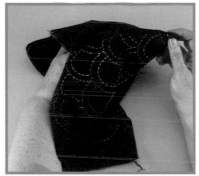

16 Turn the bag right sides out.

17 Take the open edges at the top of the bag, and fold them in 6mm (¼in). Pin them.

18 Overstitch (see page 11) along the edge of the bag front, starting at the top.

19 Continue stitching down to where the front and back of the bag meet, and up to the top part of the bag back.

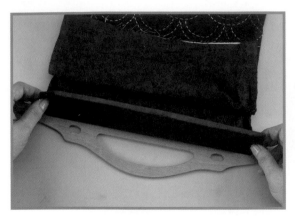

20 Place the back right side up and thread the back through the slot in the handle.

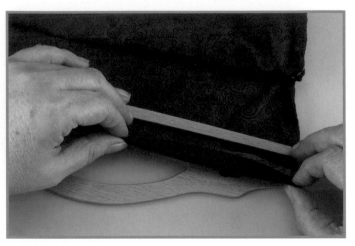

21 Fold the top edge of the bag back in 6mm (¼in).

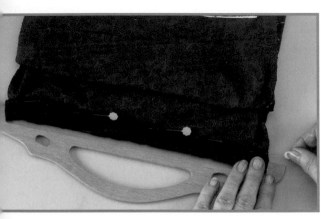

22 Fold the top down over the base of the handle and pin it in place as shown.

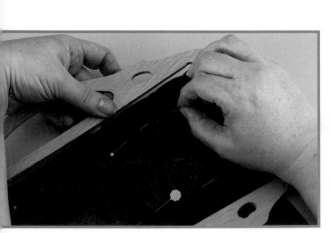

23 Slip stitch (see page 11) the folded-over edge to the bag back. Repeat steps 20 to 23 to attach the handle to the bag front.

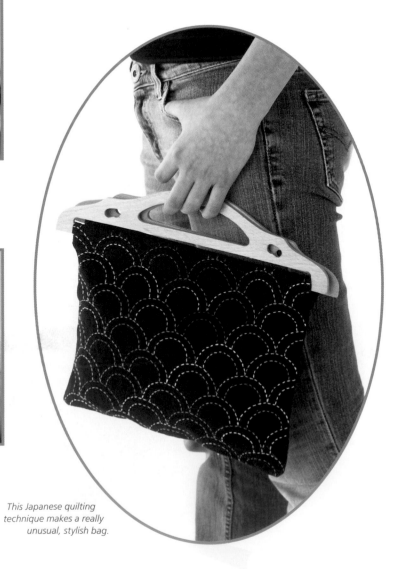

This Japanese quilting technique makes a really unusual, stylish bag.

What next?

Make a sashiko hipster belt using bright thread and decorate the ends with tassels to match.

Beady Bag

For this bright and beautiful beaded bag, choose a fabric you really like, with designs you can quilt around. Then cut out pieces for the front and back that show your favourite designs. This is called 'fussy cutting'. Some of the lining fabric will show, so choose something that will look good with your main fabric.

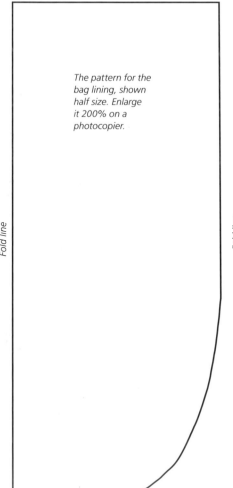

The pattern for the bag lining, shown half size. Enlarge it 200% on a photocopier.

Fold line

The pattern for the top fabric, wadding and backing fabric. The pattern is shown half size. Enlarge it 200% on a photocopier.

Fold line

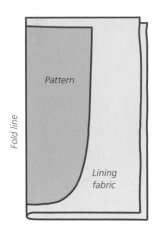

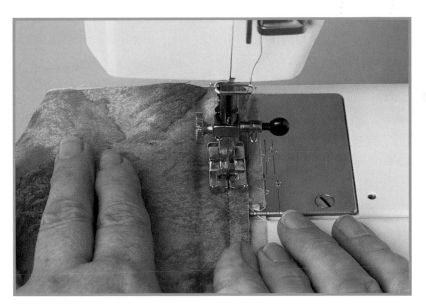

1 Cut out the enlarged patterns. Fold a piece of lining fabric in half and pin the lining pattern on top, with the edge marked 'fold' on the fold of the fabric. Draw round the pattern and cut out the shape. Repeat to make a second lining shape.

2 Use the top fabric pattern to cut out the top fabric, calico backing and wadding shapes; two of each for the front and back of the bag. Place a lining piece and a top fabric piece right sides together and use a sewing machine to sew them together, 6mm (¼in) in from the straight edges. Repeat for the back of the bag.

Stay Safe!
Ask an adult to help you with the sewing machine.

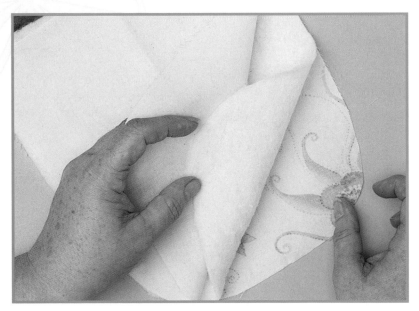

3 Open out the shapes. Make two quilt sandwiches, one for the front and one for the back. Layer the front fabric (right side down), wadding and calico backing shapes as shown.

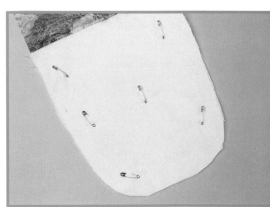

4 Safety pin the top fabric, wadding and calico backing together.

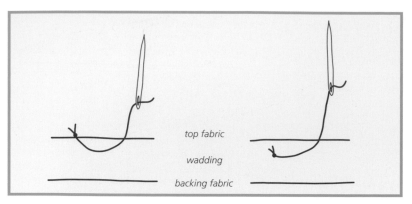

5 Thread your needle and knot the end of the thread. Place the quilt sandwich with the top fabric uppermost. Go down through the top fabric and into the wadding, near to where you want to begin quilting. Come up on the quilting line and gently pull so that the knot pops into the wadding. Now the knot will not appear on the surface.

6 Using quilting thread, sew in running stitch through the three layers around the patterns on the fabric. I sewed round the flowers and birds. Pick up beads on your needle and add them as you go. I added beads for the birds' eyes and for the flower centres.

7 Fold the lining fabric back under the quilted bag front and use an iron to press the edge as shown.

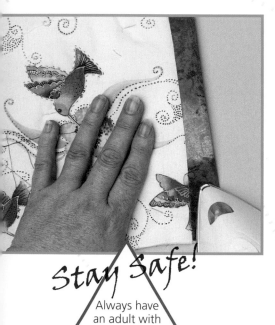

Stay Safe!

Always have an adult with you when you are ironing.

8 Repeat steps 3 to 7 to make the bag back. Take the bag front and open out the lining again. Place the bag front right side up. Open out the lining from the bag back and place it right side down on top of the bag front as shown.

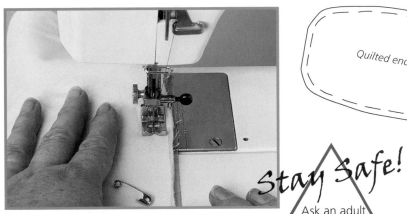

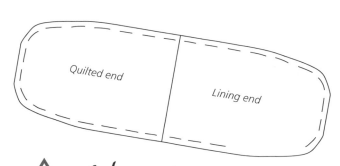

Quilted end

Lining end

Stay Safe!

Ask an adult to help you with the sewing machine.

9 Thread a sewing machine with ordinary cotton to match the main fabric. Sew right round the full oval shape, both through the quilted front and back and the lining front and back (see the diagram on the right). Leave a gap in the lining end.

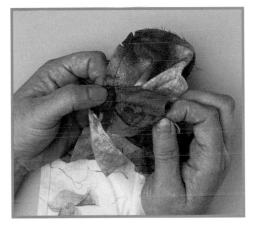

10 Pull the bag and lining through the gap in the lining so that the bag is right sides out.

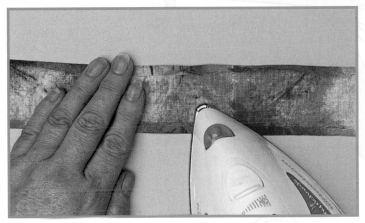

11 Take the fabric for the strap. Fold in 6mm (¼in) each side and press with an iron.

12 Fold the strap in half lengthwise. Fold in 6mm (¼in) at each end and press with the iron again. Place the wadding in the strap as shown. Tuck it under the fold at the end of the strap. Fold up the bottom half of the strap to cover the wadding.

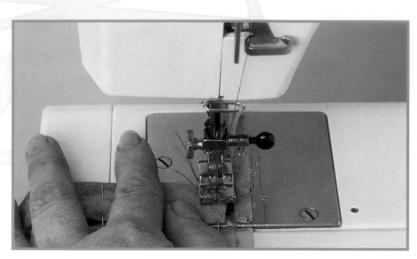

13 Pin all round the edges of the strap and then sew round it with the sewing machine.

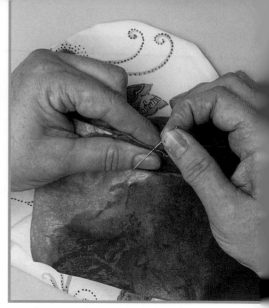

14 Slip stitch (see page 11) the gap you left in the bag lining.

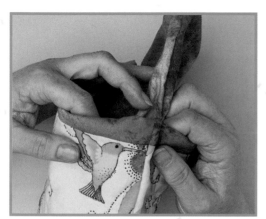

15 Push the lining inside the bag.

Choose fabulous fabrics and bright little beads for a beautiful Beady Bag.

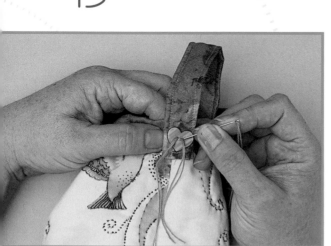

16 Pin the strap to the bag at the side seam. Attach it using a heart-shaped button with doubled thick orange thread and the tie and buttons technique (see page 12).

What next?

Why not make a little bag or purse to clip on to your belt hook?

Cat Wall Hanging

You will need

Plain blue backing fabric, 45.7 x 33cm (18 x 13in)

Cotton and polyester 80/20 mix wadding, 45.7 x 45.7cm (18 x 18in)

Purple top fabric, 45.7 x 33cm (18 x 13in)

Pink fabric, 45.7 x 12.6cm (18 x 5in)

Check fabric, ¼m (10in)

Yellow fabric for scruffy flower 20.3 x 7.6cm (8 x 3in)

Scraps for flowers

Pink, green, red and turquoise sewing threads

Thick variegated threads in orange/yellow, orange/brown, pink, yellow and pale green

Small and three large buttons

Florist wire

Fusible web

Fabric adhesive spray

Safety pins and needles

Dowelling, 55cm (21¾in)

Beige felt

Permanent marker, pencil and compasses

Scissors and pinking shears

Ribbon

Scrap card

This is a fun project that you could easily make in a day. It uses those precious buttons that people save. This type of quilt is called a 'scruffy' quilt, because it has no <u>binding</u> round the edge, so the rough edges show. You can be really creative with this type of quilt – let your imagination fly!

Start

Finish

The patterns for the Cat Wall Hanging, shown half size. Enlarge them to 200 per cent on a photocopier.

Stay Safe!

Always have an adult with you when you are ironing.

Use fabric adhesive spray near an open door or window.

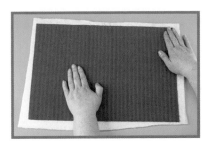

2 Place the wadding on top and smooth it down. Spray the wadding and place the top fabric on top, right side up.

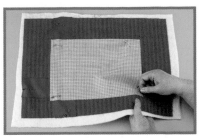

3 Place the pink strips where you want them; they look best off-centre as shown. Place the check fabric on top. Pin everything in place using safety pins.

1 Place the backing fabric face down and spray it with fabric adhesive spray. Follow the instructions on the can.

4 Thread a needle with the thick variegated pink thread. Go in at the bottom right-hand corner of the check fabric, leaving a 12cm (4¾in) tail at the end. Sew round the check fabric in large running stitch, 1cm (³/₈in) from the edge.

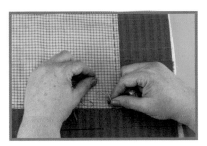

5 Leave a 12cm (4¾in) tail at the end, and tie the two tails in a bow.

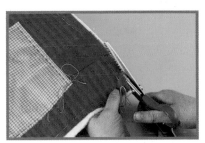

6 Sew around the wall hanging 2cm (¾in) from the edge in the same way, using the thick orange/yellow thread. Tie bows wherever you run out of thread. Trim round the edge of the quilt sandwich using pinking shears.

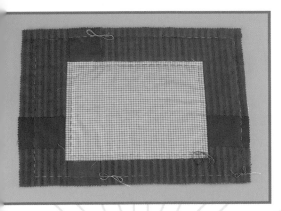

The wall hanging should now look like this.

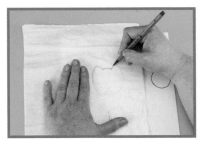

7 Place a sheet of fusible web, smooth side up over the enlarged patterns. Trace the cat pieces in pencil.

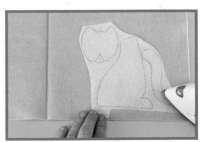

8 Cut roughly round the edges of the cat shapes. Place the fusible web on the beige felt and press with an iron, following the instructions for your fusible web.

9 Cut out the beige shapes, cutting carefully along the lines.

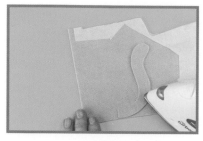

10 Peel off the backing from the tail shape. Place it on another piece of beige felt, fusible web side down. Press with an iron.

11 Cut out the shape so that you have a double thickness felt tail.

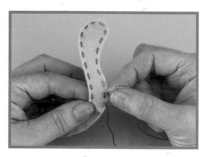

12 Sew round the tail in running stitch using the thick orange/brown variegated thread.

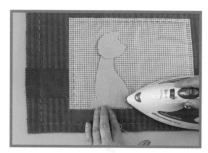

13 Peel off the backing from the head and body shapes of the cat, and place them sticky side down as shown. Press with the iron.

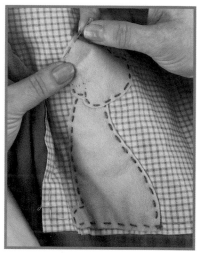

14 Sew round the head and body of the cat in running stitch, using the thick orange/brown thread.

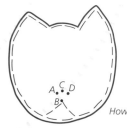

A. C. D
B.

How to sew the cat's nose.

15 To finish the cat's face, you need to sew the nose. See the diagram above. Bring the needle up at A and go down at B.

16 Come up at C and go down at B again.

17 Come up at D and go down again at B.

18 Secure the sewing at the back of the wall hanging with two little stitches through the backing fabric only.

19 Place the cat's tail and the button. Knot the end of the orange/brown thread and come up from the back through the tail and the button. Sew the button on.

20 Draw a 12.7cm (5in) circle on card, using compasses.

21 Draw round the card template on the wrong side of the pink fabric, using pencil.

22 Thread the needle with a long pink thread. Turn the edges of the pink circle in 6mm (¼in) and sew around the circle in running stitch.

23 Pull the thread tight to gather the edges of the circle. Secure with two or three overstitches. This shape is known as a Suffolk puff.

24 Trace two small circles, two large circles and two stars (see page 38) on to the fusible web. Place the shapes on orange fabric. Press with the iron and cut the shapes out.

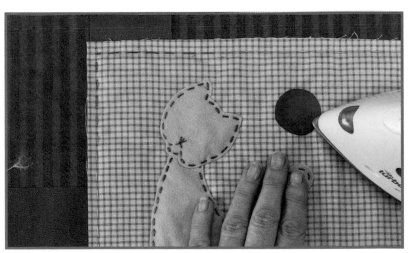

25 Peel off the backing paper from the fusible web. Place the circle above the cat's tail and press it in place with the iron.

26 Come up from the back and blanket stitch (see page 13) round the edge of the orange circle, using the pale green thread.

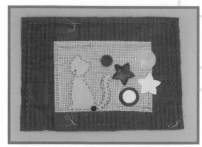

27 Attach all the other elements in the same way. Blanket stitch round the purple star and the small yellow circle using matching threads.

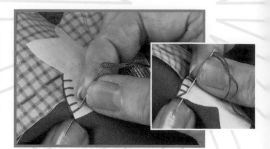

28 Sew in blanket stitch round the yellow star. When you reach the corner, go back into the same hole and out to the point. Then go back in the same hole again and out to the edge to turn the corner.

29 Running stitch round the green circle using pink variegated thread.

The wall hanging with the shapes attached and stitched.

30 Take the strip of yellow fabric for the scruffy flower and fold it in half lengthwise. Press along the fold with the iron.

3I Thread the needle with a long piece of yellow thread and knot the end. Sew in running stitch all along the raw edges. Do not trim the thread at the end.

32 Cut a fringe in the folded strip. Cut every 6mm (¼in), from the folded edge up to 6mm (¼in) from the stitched edge.

33 Pull the thread carefully.

35 Attach the scruffy flower using the tie and buttons technique (see page 12).

34 Join the end of the strip to the beginning with two overstitches (see page 11). This makes the scruffy flower shape.

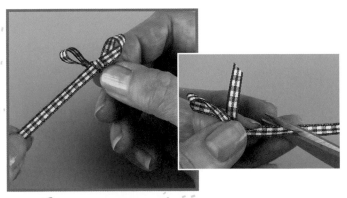

36 Take a long piece of ribbon and tie it in a bow. Trim the ends.

37 Stitch the ribbon to the cat's neck using red thread.

43

TOP TIP

Practise drawing the cat's face on paper and on scrap felt first.

38 Draw the face on the cat using permanent marker.

39 Cut three 15cm (6in) lengths of florist wire using old scissors. Holding the end with your thumb, wrap the wire round a pencil to make a spiral. Make three spirals.

40 Thread the needle with turquoise thread and knot the end. Come up from the back and do a few stitches to hold the spiral in place. Repeat for the other two.

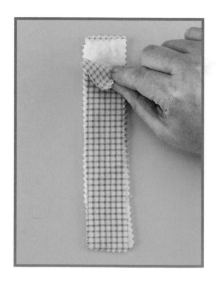

41 Use pinking shears to cut six 21.5 x 3.8cm (8½ x 1½in) check fabric strips for the tabs. Cut three strips of wadding the same size. Make a quilt sandwich with a fabric strip right side down, then a wadding strip, then a fabric strip right side up.

42 Pin the sandwich together. Thread a needle with thick variegated pink thread. Hide the knot inside the sandwich (see page 34.)

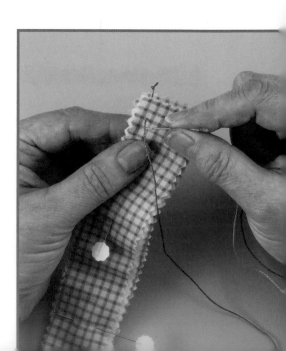

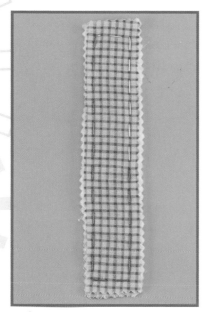

43 Sew in running stitch all round the edge of the tab. Make three tabs following steps 40 to 42.

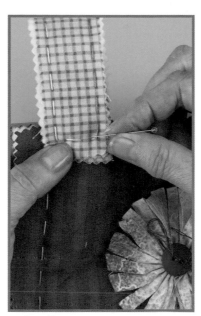

44 Fold a tab in half and place both ends at the front of the wall hanging, on the sewing line as shown. Pin it in place.

45 Place a large button in front of the tab ends. Thread the needle with doubled thick variegated orange/brown thread. Go in to one of the button's holes leaving a 5cm (2in) tail.

46 Sew around the four holes leaving a 5cm (2in) tail at the end. Tie a double knot and trim. Attach all three tabs in the same way.

47 Use the tie and buttons technique and pink variegated thread to attach the Suffolk puff flower. Attach buttons to the centres of all the other shapes.

Hang the finished wall hanging from the dowelling rod. This project is a great opportunity to raid the fabric scrap bag and delve into the button box for forgotten treasures.

What next?

You can really use your imagination with these wall hangings. Make your favourite pet instead of the cat, and go wild with scruffy flowers!

More books to read

Kids Start Quilting by Alex Anderson, C & T Publishing, 2002
Kids Can Quilt by Dorothy Stapleton, Quarto, 2004
Kids Quilt Together, Kathy Emmel, C & T Publishing, 2006

Glossary

Binding A strip of fabric sewn on to cover the edges of a quilt.

Crusaders These were fighters from Christian countries who went to fight in the Middle East to get the Holy Land back from Muslim Turks between the 11th and 13th centuries AD.

Fusible web This is a type of adhesive for sticking fabrics together. You iron it on and peel off the paper backing.

Patchwork This craft involves sewing together small pieces of fabric into a larger design, which is then often quilted.

Pioneers Settlers in a new land, in this case, America.

Quilting A method of sewing or tying two layers of fabric together with a layer of padding in between.

Sashiko A Japanese style of quilting with running stitch patterns on dark blue fabric.

Shadow quilting Small pieces of fabric are placed on a backing fabric, with a transparent fabric such as voile on top. You then stitch round the design to attach the layers together.

Variegated thread This has patches of different colours or different shades of one colour.

Wadding The layer of padding that goes on the inside of a quilt sandwich. In the US it is called 'batting'.

Index

bag 8, 9, 11, 25, 26–31, 32–37
  make-up bag 25
beads 4, 8, 17, 34, 37
belt 31
button 4, 8, 12, 14, 16, 18, 24, 36, 38, 41, 45, 46

fabric 6, 8, 9, 10, 11, 13, 14, 18, 19, 21, 26, 32, 33, 34, 35, 37, 38, 39, 41, 46
felt 6, 13, 14, 15, 38, 39, 40
flower 6, 8, 13, 14, 15, 16, 18, 24, 34, 45
fusible web 9, 38, 39, 40, 41

needle 7, 10, 11, 14, 18, 20, 21, 26, 27, 34, 38, 39, 41, 43, 44

patchwork 4, 5, 18
patterns 4, 6, 12, 14, 26, 27, 32, 33, 34, 38, 39

quilt sandwich 4, 6, 9, 10, 19, 21, 33, 34, 39, 44

ribbon 8, 38, 43

sashiko 26–31
scruffy flower 38, 42, 43, 47
scruffy quilt 38

sewing machine 7, 26, 28, 29, 33, 35, 36
shadow quilting 6, 14, 16
stitch 4, 6, 7, 10, 11, 13, 16, 19, 24, 41
  blanket stitch 13, 42
  glove stitch 13, 16
  overstitch 11, 13, 20, 22, 23, 29, 41, 43
  running stitch 10, 12, 15, 18, 20, 21, 26, 27, 34, 39, 40, 41, 42, 43, 45
  slip stitch 11, 30, 36
Suffolk puff 41, 45

thread 7, 8, 10, 11, 12, 14, 15, 16, 19, 20, 22, 23, 24, 26, 27, 31, 32, 34, 36, 38, 39, 40, 41, 42, 43, 44, 45
tie and buttons 12, 36, 43, 45
top fabric 4, 6, 10

voile 6, 14, 15

wadding 6, 10, 18, 19, 21, 32, 33, 34, 35, 38, 39, 44
wall hanging 4, 6, 8, 9, 10, 12, 13, 38–47